*Why Your Financial
Advisor Might Be
Hazardous to Your
Wealth and What
You Can Do About It*

WALL STREET'S GRAND DECEPTION

Copyright © 2022 Contango Publishing

All rights reserved. No part of this publication may be reproduced, distributed, or transmitted in any form or by any means, including photocopying, recording, or other electronic or mechanical methods, without the prior written permission of the publisher, except in the case of brief quotations embodied in critical reviews and certain other noncommercial uses permitted by copyright law. For permission requests, write to the publisher, addressed "Attention: Permissions Coordinator," at the address below.

marketing@syfft.io
ISBN: 979-8-9866159-0-5 (paperback)
ISBN: 979-8-9866159-1-2 (ebook)

Ordering Information:
Special discounts are available on quantity purchases by corporations, associations, and others. For details, contact marketing@syfft.io.

For Alexander
1968 - 1986

CONTENTS

Preface vii
Introduction.. ix
Chapter 1   Why I Wrote This Guide.......................... 1
Chapter 2   Yes, Wall Street Lies to You 13
Chapter 3   Expert Advisor or Slick Salesperson?....... 19
Chapter 4   Behind Wall Street's Facade................... 33
Chapter 5   Misconduct—Misconduct Everywhere... 41
Chapter 6   How to Protect Your Money and
            Your Future 63
Appendix: A Deeper Dive Into Investment
            Reporting 77
Acknowledgments.. 91

PREFACE

In July of 2017, Advisor Perspectives published some revealing data from a focus group comprised of affluent investors. When asked what was most important to them about the investment reports provided by their financial advisor, they said the following:

- 27 percent answered that they wanted better fee disclosure.

- 26 percent responded that they wished their reporting was simpler and easier to understand.

- But a whopping 48 percent replied, "something else."[1]

---

[1] David Thompson and Benjamin Gross, "What Investors Want Most in Investment Reporting," Advisor Perspectives, July 24, 2017, https://www.advisorperspectives.com/articles/2017/07/24/what-investors-want-most-in-investment-reporting.

Realizing they were onto something, David Thompson and Benjamin Gross, the study's authors, delved deeper.

It turns out that the most important thing to the 48 percent was the issue of trusting the performance reporting they were given. Most of the respondents were uneasy about what they considered an apparent conflict of interest: their financial advisor reviewing their own results. Some compared the financial advisor-produced reports to a school report card created by the student.

Seeking to clarify these trust issues further, the study asked, "How confident are you that an unbiased third party would get the same results as your financial advisor when calculating certain performance metrics?" The study's participants were then provided with five categories. In each category, between 30 and 40 percent of the respondents were not highly confident that an independent third party would produce the same performance results as their financial advisor given the same portfolio data.

The wealth management industry's leadership read the data. They and their marketing departments understood what would happen if they removed their firms' conflicts-of-interests and provided greater transparency. And the inevitable followed—Wall Street continued with business as usual.

INTRODUCTION

No enemy is worse than bad advice.
—Sophocles[2]

Wall Street is a uniquely American institution built on power and money. Oh, and one other thing. Deceit.

Turn on the television and you'll see expertly crafted commercials about the wealth management industry's devotion to your financial security. Unfortunately, the reality is very different. A 2015 seminal study by the Executive Office of the President of the United States

---

[2] Sophocles, *Electra* in *Greek Tragedies 2: Aeschylus: The Libation Bearers; Sophocles: Electra; Euripides: Iphigenia among the Taurians, Electra, The Trojan Women*, trans. David Grene and Richard Lattimore (Chicago: University of Chicago Press, 2013), 92.

raised a lot of eyebrows when it analyzed 10 academic research papers that studied the cost of "conflicted investment advice:"

> For the saver in this example who rolls over her 401(k) balance at 45, the combined effect of a 17 percent loss leading up to retirement and a 12 percent loss after retirement is an overall loss of more than 25 percent. That is, as a result of conflicted investment advice, the feasible retirement withdrawals for this saver fall by more than 25 percent compared to what would have been possible with unconflicted advice.[3]

At first glance, the report may seem to hold a low regard for the full-service financial advisor, but they don't tell you if using a discount brokerage improves portfolio performance.

So should you walk into a full-service brokerage like a Merrill Lynch or Morgan Stanley, or open up an online account at a discount brokerage like a TD Ameritrade/Schwab or Robin Hood? To answer this question, we'll take a bit of a detour.

America has never been as fat and unhealthy as it is today. At the same time, the diet and exercise industry

---

[3] "The Effects of Conflicted Investment Advice on Retirement Savings," Executive Office of the President of the United States, February 2015, 18, https://obamawhitehouse.archives.gov/sites/default/files/docs/cea_coi_report_final.pdf.

INTRODUCTION

has exploded and is a larger part of our economy than ever. What gives? The diet and exercise industry is giving good advice and Americans want to live healthier lives.

A lot of Americans do live healthy lives. They eat right and exercise. But many have been unable to adopt that lifestyle and constantly battle with their bathroom scale.

It's the same in the investment world.

Let me introduce you to two actual people: Mary (her real name) and Mark (a pseudonym for reasons that will be clear in a bit). Mary is someone I have known for most of my life. She graduated from college and had a career in the federal government in a position that would be classified today as an administrative assistant. At every chance, Mary maxed out her retirement contributions. Additionally, Mary set aside 10 percent of her net pay and invested it into 10-year government bonds—generally regarded as the safest security in the world.

Mary never married. When she retired after 40 years, Mary had a seven-figure nest egg. In her retirement years, Mary, a devout Christian, was able to donate generously to the less fortunate people in her community. When she passed away, she left enough money to pay off the mortgages of her nieces and nephews. Last, she set up a trust for one child in particular, a special needs child who had tragically lost their father.

Contrast Mary with Mark, a Goldman Sachs executive vice president. Mark is still working at high levels in the investment industry, so I changed his name.

I first met Mark in New York City's Harvard Club. Our host was, and remains, famous in the annals of the investment community, and he was trying to bring us onboard his latest entrepreneurial effort.

During the lunch, Mark asked me how my personal investing was going.

At this point, I have to take another detour and explain to you the differences in social graces between professional and amateur investors. When the market is going gangbusters, like during the late 1990s, amateur investors will brag about their successes. Professional investors rarely swap success stories with their peers. More often, professional investors will engagingly tell a story about when they got smacked down with a loss they did not see coming. Professional investors bragging is not entertaining to other professional investors. But telling a story of how you missed something, and it ended up biting you on your rear-end, now those stories are usually highly entertaining to other professional investors. So the moral of this detour is that if you hear someone bragging about their investing success in a social setting, chances are great they are not a professional investor.

I replied truthfully. My stock picking left a lot to be desired. I have good skill avoiding big drawdowns but usually share too little in the market upswings.

Nodding his head, Mark laughed. "Let me tell you a

quick story," he said. "One afternoon I decided to review my IRA portfolio's performance with our internal software. Turns out my personal investing was pretty awful. So after the day was over, I got into a cab and went to the nearest Merrill Lynch office and opened an account. I'm much better off for having done that." We both laughed.

You might wonder how somebody could be great at investing billions and billions of dollars but somehow be less than average at investing their own money. It's not unusual to be an expert at something and not take your own advice. How many therapists save hundreds of marriages each year only to find their own marriage ending up in divorce court? How many doctors prescribe lifestyle changes to their patients that they themselves fail to follow when afflicted with a similar condition?

A thousand people could receive world-class diet and exercise advice. But how many would benefit from it? Now what if you gave those same thousand people a personal chef and exercise coach? Do you think that might increase the number of people that would benefit from diet and exercise advice?

Sure, you can use the discount brokers. And many people will be successful using them. They will save a lot of money on trades. But I believe more people would benefit from a skilled financial advisor guiding them through the financial challenges of their life.

That said, the benefit you receive from a diet and exercise coach can be quantified in the level of your physical fitness and your bathroom scale. Both are objective measures. You need a financial advisor that produces results, not one that simply holds your hand and makes you feel good when you meet with them.

Finding a really good financial advisor has been made difficult by the industry. They would rather you select a financial advisor based on their billion-dollar marketing campaigns.

Most financial advisors are simply ill-equipped to help you achieve your goals for two reasons:

1. They don't have the skills, experience, and training.
2. Their employer's business model is designed to win at your expense.

Up to 90 percent of financial advisors fail in the first three years.[4] What is interesting is that the threshold for career longevity is not investment skill. It is how much money you can bring through the firms' front doors. And those financial advisors that fail? The money they have brought into the firm normally stays with the firm for many years after that financial advisor has left. Wall Street has the economics of client acquisition down to

---

[4] "11 Reasons Why You'll Fail as a Financial Advisor," The Advisor Coach, accessed March 15, 2022, https://www.theadvisorcoach.com/7-reasons-youll-fail-as-a-financial-advisor.html#:~:text=Up%20to%2090%25%20of%20financial,a%20stepping%20stone%20to%20success.

a fine science.[5]

Wall Street doesn't want you to worry about your financial advisor's investment skills or ethics. But when it comes to managing your wealth, could there be a more important question?

If you're one of the millions of Americans who work with a financial advisor, you need the cold hard facts, not the version Wall Street wants you to see.

That's why I wrote this guide—to arm you with the knowledge to find high-quality, ethical help, and protect you and your family from shady, unethical financial advisors.

We are launching FinancialAdvisorCheck.com in 2022 to produce a confidential, third-party performance report on your investment portfolio without the knowledge of your investment advisor. It's the kind of guidance I wish my family would have had when I was a boy.

---

[5] "What's Life Like as a Financial Advisor? Depends on Your Pain Tolerance," Financial Samurai, August 12, 2021, https://www.financialsamurai.com/the-life-of-a-financial-advisor/.

CHAPTER 1
Why I Wrote This Guide

The door to my brother's room wouldn't budge.

I knocked, turned the knob, and pushed my shoulder into the wood—nothing. Something awful had happened that I believe was directly connected to my father putting his trust in a shady financial advisor and our family's savings getting wiped out.

My father was a successful physician who grew up in Greece but later immigrated to the United States. Before that, he survived the Nazi occupation of Athens and endured combat on the front lines of the Greek Civil War that followed World War II. But even lessons learned from these life-changing events could not protect him from the wiles of Wall Street.

Wall Street in the '70s

The year was 1978. Inflation was surging, the economy was in a recession, and unemployment was reaching highs not seen since the Great Depression. With stocks treading water, commodities like food, oil, and precious metals were the hot investments.

Wall Street firms hired young, energetic brokers and handed them a telephone and a long list of phone numbers. These investor lists were hot properties, often worth thousands of dollars. "Smile and dial" was the mantra of the moment. The Wall Street firms even paid sales experts to craft a pitch that would build trust and motivate people to invest.

One of the more infamous examples from that era was the Orange Juice pitch. The name not only refers to the target investment—it also references the location where it was designed to be practiced. Central Florida was not only the center of the orange juice industry—it was also home to millions of newly-retired, wealthy professionals.

The Con

The Orange Juice strategy begins with a large phone list consisting of about 1,000 names of wealthy people. The list is then divided into two equal parts. Half the brokers get 500 names to whom they would pitch the "bullish" theme. The idea is that their orange juice expert has analyzed current market conditions and proclaimed orange juice futures to be a "strong buy." The other 500 people got the exact opposite advice, the "bearish" theme. They are told that their orange juice expert believes the market is signaling a "strong sell."

Potential clients are asked to buy options on orange juice futures to take advantage of the expert's insight. The cost? They will pay a $250 per trade commission on the investment. Expensive? Yes. But it's easily rationalized by having to pay for the services of this elite expert.

In 30 days, the orange juice market has gone one of two ways. Half of the new clients made money and are happy about their investment. Or if they didn't buy, they would have been impressed that the call was accurate. The other half? That list is quickly discarded.

Those remaining on the "winning" list are called back. "Remember our expert's call on the orange juice market? Well, he (or she) was right again, as we expected." The financial advisor then quotes the current price of OJ with confidence. Even the most skeptical retiree would find greed taking hold. Only now the commission is not $250—it is $1,000 per trade.

The list continues to be split, with each half receiving either a buy or sell recommendation. The cost of the commission continues to increase, too. The con continues until its inevitable endpoint: angry investors vowing never to take investment advice over the phone again. But the brokerage receives a massive return on the money it used to buy that phone list. And that elite orange juice expert? Never existed.

Dad's Unfortunate Experience

My father was not a part of the Orange Juice pitch. Instead, the pitch was about another commodity: silver. I don't know exactly what that financial advisor told my father in 1979, but I bet it went something like this:

> Look, doctor, if you had invested in the stock market at the beginning of the decade, you would have a profit of exactly zero dollars. However, if you invested $1 in silver, that dollar would now be worth over $20. You're a doctor, and that means you are a smart man. Which investment sounds better to you?

Now, commodities are not necessarily bad investments, but they can be very volatile, so they are not well-suited for retirement investing. Instead, a quality advisor would just put a tiny fraction of your retirement funds into this asset class. But that didn't stop Dad's broker. He urged my father to invest his entire retirement account, and then some.

In less than two years, silver fell from a high of around $32 back to almost $6. My father was nearly wiped out. In less than two years, the broker essentially destroyed everything my father had worked his professional life to build.

Wall Street's Real Skill Set

You can see a strong skill set in the financial industry of the 1970s. Unfortunately, it wasn't wealth-building for its customers—it was pure sales, backed by a carefully crafted illusion.

That commodities broker's sales skill, masquerading as professional financial advice, brought devastating stress to my family. Our lifestyle went from comfort to survival. My father turned to alcohol, and my parents' fights became more frequent and nastier.

The erosion of our family's financial and emotional stability took a tremendous toll on my brother. We were not fully aware of his depression until April 8, 1986. On that fateful night, I arrived home from college and found my brother's door locked. My knocking, then banging, brought no response. Panic inside me grew until I started using my shoulder to break the door down. When the door finally gave way, I found my 18-year-old brother lying on his bed, dead. My father's pistol was still in his hand.

I have always believed that absent that broker's actions, my brother would still be alive.

Searching for Answers

Two days after we buried my brother, I went down into the basement of my parents' house looking for old brokerage statements. I searched for the broker's name whose incompetence pushed my family into the dire financial situation that laid the groundwork for my brother's suicide. I never found his name—my parents wouldn't reveal it, either. No doubt they were afraid of what I might do. The anger burned inside of me like a raging wildfire.

Research by the National Institutes of Health and other institutions have linked a family's financial stress to damage to children's emotional health.[6] A 2004 report by Christopher G. Davis and Janet Mantler of Carleton University states the following:

> Children of financially stressed parents tend to be more prone to mental health problems, depression, loneliness, and are more emotionally sensitive…. They are less sociable and more distrustful and are more likely to feel excluded by their peers, especially if they are girls…. Boys of financially stressed parents are likely to exhibit low self-esteem, to show behavior problems in school, and be susceptible to negative peer pressure and alcohol and drug problems. … financial stress was associated with more

---

[6] Christopher G. Davis and Janet Mantler, "The Consequences of Financial Stress for Individuals, Families, and Society, Centre for Research on Stress, Coping, and Well-Being, Department of Psychology, Carleton College, March 31, 2004, https://www.researchgate.net/publication/229052873_The_Consequences_of_Financial_Stress_for_Individuals_Families_and_Society.

> symptoms of depression, antisocial behavior, and impulsive behavior in children.[7]

I ended up turning my rage into purpose. I was 22 years old at the time of my brother's death, and I made an important decision: I would pursue a career in the investment world to help safeguard and carefully manage people's hard-earned money. I'd make a difference.

The Most Prized Skill Is Not Investing Acumen

I dove into the financial industry headfirst, landing a job at a London-based global investment bank after earning a bachelor's in economics and a master's degree in finance. I learned quickly that you have to have strong investment skills to succeed in the institutional environment. And you couldn't just talk about your returns—you had to prove it.

Institutional clients demanded a track record of your historical investment results to earn their business. If sufficiently impressed, they invited you to present to their investment committee, made up of degreed, experienced investment professionals. During this presentation, your historical investment performance comes under intense scrutiny. Then, if you're fortunate enough to win the business, they require you to continue reporting your performance to ensure they get what they paid for.

---

[7] Ibid.

In other words, they demanded accountability. And if you don't deliver acceptable results, the business is yanked, usually with nothing more than a phone call. It's not personal—it's business, and protecting hard-earned money was prioritized.

Preparing for these meetings was intense. You knew that the people we were presenting to were going to be provided analysis from freshly minted MBAs hoping to make an impression on their superiors. These young analysts had every motivation to drill down and find the weakness in our investing approach.

You had to know how your funds performed in up markets, down markets, rising interest rate environments, and falling interest rate environments. Our risk management was questioned—how would we know we were wrong about a pick? Those are just a few of the situations you could be asked about. You could also be asked about how geopolitical events might affect your fund's performance. The questions are challenging, and the stress level is high. Millions of dollars in annual management fees are at stake.

Should you be fortunate enough to win the business, the oversight does not end. Institutions now routinely demand access to your firm's servers to download all of their funds' daily information. At the end of every day, your client will know what they own, what they bought, what they sold, and especially the value of their investment. Should the performance of their funds fail to reach the standards they expected when they hired you, a caution will be given. If performance does not improve over the next six months or year, it would not be unexpected to have a transfer order from the institution asking for their money back. That activity brings additional unwelcome factors with it—the most damaging being the rumor mill whispers that a major institution pulled their money from your fund. A rumor like that will encourage other institutions to more closely review their own funds' performance under your stewardship. It's not unusual for funds to suffer a snowball effect after a high-profile institution has redeemed their investment.

After spending years working with these institutions as well as investment banks, mutual fund families, and hedge funds, I was ready to use my knowledge to help real people. So, I returned to my hometown, the Virginia suburbs of Washington D.C., and I landed a job as a financial advisor at the local branch of a prestigious international wealth management firm. With my experience helping large institutions preserve and grow assets, who would not trust me with their money? I could not have been more naive.

After a few weeks, I realized I had entered a completely different world: one of sales pressure and quotas. Instead of focusing on the client's results, the firm groomed us to be salespeople who were judged by the amount of client money we could bring through the front door.

Nobody asked what I learned while working with

some of the world's top financial institutions. No one asked to see my investing track record. The only skill that mattered here was salesmanship.

This realization was not frustrating or depressing. It was soul crushing. It brought back memories of my father's investment losses. After many years, the industry had not changed. The focus was still on bringing in new money and generating fees for the firm. They had no interest in producing investment professionals.

Two Different Standards

You, as a client, are expected to "trust the expert" and are given no visibility into your advisor's skill set. You see how that turned out for my family.

Sadly, these types of bad outcomes are all too common. There are thousands of complaints filed against retail advisors every year. The most common involve a failure to place the client's interest first or a failure to adequately supervise the firm's advisors.

Advisors and firms were penalized over $82 million in 2020 alone.[8] That's not even counting the many situations that likely go unreported, undetected, or unenforced—like my family's.

It's a jungle out there for an unsuspecting investor.

---

[8] "Statistics," FINRA, accessed February 27, 2022, https://www.finra.org/media-center/statistics.

Even worse, everyday people are made to feel like kings in this jungle—but they are actually the prey.

While it sounds outrageous, it is purely business as usual in today's wealth management industry. It's all about creating the illusion that your advisor is a skilled investment professional while pushing that same advisor to bring more clients and assets in the door.

CHAPTER 2
Yes, Wall Street Lies to You

Penn & Teller, the famed magic duo, created a television show called *Penn & Teller: Fool Us*. In each episode, a professional magician performs their signature trick for Penn & Teller. If they can effectively fool these two masters of illusion, the individual wins a trophy and appears in their Las Vegas show.

While the show is purely for entertainment, it's not that far off from what you see in today's retail investment industry. You already saw how that played out in the Orange Juice pitch of the 1970s. But believe it or not, that's just the tip of the iceberg. While today's shenanigans may be less blatant, sadly, new and different tactics are widespread.

Let's take a closer look so you can be aware of modern-day Wall Street tactics and traps.

What's in a Name?

Decades ago you dealt with a stockbroker. That stockbroker charged you commissions. When you bought a stock, you got charged a commission—it was easy to see.

Their role was clear, but over time, the title of stockbroker lost its luster. People especially lost trust in brokers after the dot-com crash. So the industry, aware of the negative implication of the term, had to get creative. They started calling themselves "financial advisors," "wealth managers," or "registered representatives."

Not surprisingly, these name games confuse people. And they should, because there are two different types of legal standards out there for financial advice:

1. **Fiduciary advice**, where a financial professional is legally required to put your interests first. This is what most people think of when they hear the term "advisor."

2. **Suitability**, which is very different. According to Investopedia, "Suitability refers to an ethical, enforceable standard regarding investments that financial professionals are held to when dealing with clients."[9]

It should shock you that it's completely legal for these

---

[9] James Chen, "Suitable (Suitability)," Investopedia, updated October 10, 2021, https://www.investopedia.com/terms/s/suitable.asp.

stockbrokers (now called "advisors," too) to recommend a product to you that pays them higher commissions, as long as it is generally "suitable" for your needs.

Building Wealth for Who?

You don't have to be Penn & Teller to see the problem here. You think you're paying for real advice, but instead, you may very well be getting a product recommendation. And that product recommendation probably just costs you more with no other benefit. So it's not hard to imagine where that $17 billion annual cost to investors originates.

As Penn & Teller would say, "Fool us." Unless you know to question which legal standard that particular advisor is subject to, you may be the one getting fooled. This, of course, is by design—this confusion is intended to keep people in the dark.

Consumer advocates have been trying to get legislation passed for years to prevent this abuse of the title "financial advisor." They did have a small victory in 2020 when the SEC issued a ruling known as "Regulation Best Interest," which instructed brokerages to better define their standards of conduct (fiduciary responsibilities and conflicts of interest) and contractual obligations with regards to their clients.[10] But the lobbying power of Wall Street has fought it and also shifted toward alternative titles such as "financial consultant" or "retirement consultant." It's still a gray area, so as always, buyer beware.

Focused on Sales, Not on Your Results

Unfortunately, it gets even worse. In this case, it's not usually the individual financial advisors that are the problem. It's the actual business model most of the industry is built on.

Many wealth management firms impose sales quotas, subjecting even the most ethical advisors to corrupt temptations. They may have to recommend high cost products if they want to keep their jobs.

That happens all the time. One common recruitment strategy from the big firms is to lure advisors from competitors with large signing bonuses. These bonuses can range from $50,000 to often up to $1 million or more. While they are called bonuses, there is a catch: these big paydays come with strings attached. The advisor must achieve specific sales quotas. If they don't, they must pay back the bonus.

Sadly, this leads to these individuals feeling pressured

---

[10] Greg Iacurci, "Your Financial Advisor Might Not Actually Be an 'Advisor,'" CNBC, May 5, 2020, https://www.cnbc.com/2020/05/05/sec-rule-requires-brokers-to-stop-calling-themselves-advisors.html.

to increase revenues any way they can. Often that involves providing advice that isn't in their customer's best interest. Individuals who can't or don't meet these quotas often end up filing bankruptcy and looking for other work, with the firm keeping the clients the advisor worked so hard to acquire.

An article by Jeffrey Meitrodt in the *Star-Tribune* describes this situation well and has reported this practice is on the rise.[11] According to regulatory records, Ameriprise, the nation's fifth largest investment firm, spent $152 million on recruiting in 2017, nearly triple what it spent in 2010.[12] Recruiting packages in the six figures are now typical.

One former Wells Fargo financial advisor said he felt trapped after failing to meet his production quotas. The company started docking his paycheck to recover $520,000 in bonus money.

"It incentivizes you to make bad decisions and really do things that you normally wouldn't do," said the broker, who explained that's when he started selling his customers investments that carried higher fees. He quit less than two years after joining Wells Fargo and was later ordered to repay more than $450,000 in bonus money in an arbitration proceeding, forcing him into bankruptcy.

---

[11] Jeffrey Meitrodt, "How Brokers' Big Bonuses Can Lead To Ruin," *Star-Tribune*, March 25, 2019, https://www.startribune.com/how-brokers-big-bonuses-can-lead-to-ruin/507415292/?refresh=true.

[12] https://www.startribune.com/how-brokers-big-bonuses-can-lead-to-ruin/507415292/?refresh=true

This recruiting strategy has ruined many careers. "I had a 20-year career, and I wound up delivering pizzas and driving for Uber," said another former advisor, who claimed bankruptcy after being unable to pay back $200,000 in bonuses.

That's just the employees. Think of all the clients who were sold high-fee investments due to this collective pressure—all in service of the Wall Street profit machine.

We don't need Penn & Teller to inform us that we're not seeing the whole picture. With most legal action taking place in arbitration, not much is revealed or known about this secretive world.

But as an investor, you can see this is information you need to know when your money is on the line.

CHAPTER 3
Expert Advisor or Slick Salesperson?

Most people are turned off by the traditional auto-industry business model revolving around car salespeople. In fact, a whole new industry has been spawned where you can buy a car online, primarily to avoid the high-pressure tactics you expect at dealerships.

Sadly, Wall Street's masters of deception (marketing departments) make sure that prospective clients think they are dealing with consummate investment professionals, not salespeople. But this time, the stakes are much higher: they are not dealing with a one-time car purchase. They are dealing with an individual's life savings and future financial security.

As we saw in Chapter 2, the incentive system on Wall Street is a significant problem. But it's not the only one.

A Very Low Bar

The Certified Financial Planner (CFP) Board of Standards is the investment industry's largest professional standard-setting organization and oversees about 90,000 CFP-certified investment professionals.

In 2013, the organization ran an experiment that turned into a television advertisement. Real-life disc jockey Azymyth Kaminski has no financial knowledge or training but is asked to look the part of a financial advisor. The makeover begins: gone are the long dreadlocks, earrings, and eyeliner, replaced with a sleek new haircut, tailored suit, and a sheet of investing buzzwords. Azymyth then meets with several unsuspecting people to convince them to invest with him. All but one agrees.[13]

According to *Time*, the ad "serves as a cautionary tale and fair warning to all of us: things are not always as they seem, and we'd be wise to do our homework before putting our money in the hands of just anyone."[14]

---

[13] "Certified Financial Planner TV Spot 'DJ'," iSpottv, February 3, 2014, https://www.ispot.tv/ad/7Ta1/certified-financial-planner-dj.

[14] Raisa Bruner, "Watch a DJ Go Undercover as a Financial Planner and Land Several Clients," *Time*, June 10, 2016, https://time.com/4364655/dj-undercover-financial-planner-ad/.

Even Hairdressers Require More Training

Believe it or not, that commercial is not far from what you can expect if you randomly pick a financial advisor. To quote the financial blogger Blair duQuesnay:

> The bar to hold oneself out as a financial advisor is low, shockingly low. This is all the more shocking because the stakes are so high. Clients have only one chance to save and invest for retirement. If bad advice leads to the unnecessary loss of capital, there is no time to start over.[15]

In fact, in many states, getting licensed as a hairdresser requires substantially more education and investment of time.[16] The requirement to become a financial advisor is to pass a three-hour exam and have a high school diploma. And according to another well-known financial blogger and advisor, Michael Kitces, it could be argued that even the diploma might be optional in some places.

So, while you might be working with a financial advisor with years of study and training to perfect their craft, you also just might be working with someone who plays the role well—like Azymyth Kaminski did in the CFP

---

[15] Blair duQuesnay, "Substance," The Belle Curve, February 27, 2019, https://blairbellecurve.com/substance/.
[16] Michael Kitces, "Are The Licensing and Other Requirements To Become a Financial Advisor Too Easy?" Kitces, August 24, 2015, https://www.kitces.com/blog/are-the-licensing-and-other-requirements-to-become-a-financial-advisor-too-easy/.

advertisement.

Yes, this is far different than most of us are used to in the real world. When we go to see a physician, we don't come prepared with a list of questions to see if they really have medical knowledge. With an MD behind their name, we automatically assume that they have the extensive training and credentials required to practice medicine.

Same with lawyers: we usually don't second guess whether these people have a firm grasp of the law. It is assumed.

Doing that with a financial advisor can be hazardous to your wealth.

Here again, it's the sleight of hand at work—just because someone has the title "financial advisor" behind their name doesn't mean much. They may be new to investing and never managed anyone's real-money portfolio before. Or they may be a terrible investment manager who consistently underperforms the markets.

I know it sounds strange, but the retail wealth management industry doesn't do much to prevent this. Consider this: thousands of financial advisors are fired by their firms for failure to bring in enough clients and fees to sustain their employment every year. Yet, I have never once heard of an instance of a financial advisor being dismissed because of poor investment performance.

Bottom line, in an industry that should be dominated

by the best investment managers, we find something different. We see an industry that rewards those with superior sales skills.

Producer of the Year

Firms have a name for those who get results for the firm: producer.

In fact, the leading wealth management firms specifically incentivize their advisors to produce more clients and more assets under management. If you look, you'll see financial advisors who proudly list "Producer of the Year" on their biography.

On the flip side, there is no incentive to generate the best investment results for clients. Doing so may actually get an advisor into trouble, since spending too much time with existing clients probably means not enough time spent prospecting for new clients. This concept was well-outlined over 80 years ago in the classic book, *Where are the Customers' Yachts?* by Fred Schwed Jr.[17]

Sadly, it's nothing new. Regardless, it is the reality of how these firms generate profits, so that's how they structure compensation for financial advisors.

---

[17] Fred Schwed Jr., *Where Are the Customers' Yachts? Or a Good Look at Wall Street* (Hoboken: Wiley, 2006).

Commissions and Invisible Fees

Usually, fees for professionals are straightforward. You probably pay either a flat or hourly fee for someone to do your taxes or if hire a lawyer. When you get an invoice, it clearly states their fee and how it's calculated.

Ever get one of those straightforward invoices from a financial advisor?

Ever wonder why wealth management is so different?

Part of it is by design. Because while you're building wealth, the focus is usually on percentage return. If you are generating 8 percent returns per year, for example, your money will grow faster than if you get a 2 percent return. Not just a bit faster, exponentially faster. That's the power of compound interest.

Fees Compound, Too

Here's the problem. Fees compound, too, but in the other direction. They erode your wealth. Every dollar in fees you pay is one less dollar generating interest or returns for you, now and in the future.

Wall Street has a vested interest in downplaying those fees. If most investors saw the actual fees they pay each year, they'd realize the financial damage many of these advisors are doing. Instead, clients are kept in the dark. Some account statements don't reflect total fees.

In fact, fees for the mutual funds and exchange-traded funds your advisor puts you in are typically nowhere to be found. You'd have to look them up online to find their actual cost.

Speaking of mutual fund fees, these can be expensive—although, fortunately, fees have been dropping due to competition for the past several years. Still, however, you'll find funds out there charging much more than others.

Do you get what you pay for? A 2010 study by Morningstar found just the opposite: low-cost funds usually beat out high-cost funds and are far more likely to outperform.[18]

One reason is that some of those fees may go toward things that you may not appreciate or benefit from. Some of these high-profile mutual fund families spend enormous amounts of money advertising to consumers. Here's the catch: unlike other businesses where the firm's revenues are used to fund those expenses, mutual funds are allowed to pass marketing costs on to existing fundholders through something called a "12B-1" fee.[19] That's right—the fund company charges you a fee that is earmarked to be used to fund advertising of the fund you

---

[18] Russel Kinnel, "How Expense Ratios and Star Ratings Predict Success," Morningstar, August 9, 2010, www.morningstar.com/articles/347327/how-expense-ratios-and-star-ratings-predict-success.

[19] James Chen, "12B-1 Fee," Investopedia, March 23, 2020, https://www.investopedia.com/terms/1/12b-1fees.asp.

already own. They justify this by claiming that the more investors, the greater the expenses can be distributed among them. The truth is, that thinking is laughable. It's just a way the investment industry got their client to pay for expenses so the fund's management could access larger profits. But you'd have to read the fine print in the mutual fund reporting to ferret that out.

These annual costs gradually eat away at your wealth. When all fees are factored in, many people pay more than 2 percent per year in fees to their wealth manager. Now, if the advisor is earning you far more than that percentage, that would be one thing. But very rarely do advisors document their track record. That's no surprise, since most advisors don't even match market returns.[20]

And during bear markets, if your account drops, the financial advisor still gets paid.

If your account goes up, they get paid even more when their fee is based on your assets under management. So if your account doubles, or if you get a big bonus or inheritance and add it to your account, your advisor gets paid more. But has the workload changed? Probably not.

It is shocking to learn how differently wealth management operates than other professional services.

---

[20] Justin Anderson, "Study: The Typical Investment Advisor Can't Beat the S&P 500," Yahoo! Finance, March 27, 2021, https://finance.yahoo.com/news/dont-pay-investment-adviser-beat-144400899.html.

Fool Us

Why do people tolerate this lack of transparency? In many cases, these Wall Street firms service institutional, high net-worth, and retail clients. The institutional and high net-worth clients demand transparency and accountability, so they get it. These ultra-high net-worth clients receive institutional level portfolio performance reporting. The type of analysis that enables them to conclusively determine if the advisor is earning their fees or not.

Retail clients? In most every case, they are not provided that same transparency.

Here's that sleight of hand again—out of sight, out of mind. No one puts the fees in front of you, so you don't even have a point of comparison.

Some good news: recently, more independent financial advisors are trying to change this system by turning to flat or hourly fees. Or they may charge a subscription, such as $300 per month. While this is promising, the "assets under management" fee model still dominates the industry.

Are You a Winner?

To add insult to injury, the large wealth management firms even throw extra incentives and internal sales pressure on their advisors to sell their highest fee products.

In 2016, the *New York Times* profiled a bonus program offered by Morgan Stanley that tripled the sales of a high-profit-margin loan program.[21] The firm whipped up interest among advisors by offering prizes and money. The amounts the advisors would win would escalate after they sold it to 30 clients.

So these "financial advisors" were calling people to recommend this specific product. Since the game was exciting, they probably brainstormed the best pitch to help explain why you suddenly needed the product. Would Penn & Teller have fallen for this?

From the Horse's Mouth

I discovered early that the wealth management industry could not care less if their financial advisors were skilled at investing. Instead, they simply demand that their advisors bring clients through the front door and generate fees.

As a retail advisor, part of my initial onboarding involved training at the company's global headquarters. What I most looked forward to was the welcome speech from the company's CEO. On that day, about 400 new hires gathered in the auditorium, waiting for him. He

---

[21] Paul Sullivan, "Red-Flag Time: Your Broker Offers a Can't-Miss Sales Contest," *New York Times*, October 21, 2016, https://www.nytimes.com/2016/10/22/your-money/red-flag-time-your-broker-offers-a-cant-miss-sales-contest.html.

was about 20 minutes late, and after he arrived, he told us why:

> *I'm sorry I'm late, but I was on the phone with one of our top producers out West. I'm trying to get him to use our mutual fund platforms. The problem is that when the markets go up, his clients don't participate in the market rise as much as they should. And when the markets go down, his clients lose more than the market does. But he thinks he is a great stock picker, and I can't get him away from it.*

He shook his head then raised his hands with kind of a "what can I do" smirk on his face, and everybody in the room laughed. Except me. I was shocked. Here was the CEO of one of the world's premier wealth management firms. He was telling hundreds of brand-new employees that he did not have the power to dictate a course of action to one of his financial advisors that would benefit the firm's clients. How could this be?

The financial advisor in question was one of the firm's top producers. That meant he earned the firm millions of dollars every year. If that advisor was ordered to take an action that he didn't like, he could easily walk across the street to a competitor and take all his clients with him. So, the firm's management looked the other way even though they knew the advisor's investment decisions harmed their clients.

That's the problem in action. It's a direct conflict—investors value financial advisors that excel at investment management. Wealth management firms value something else: advisors who excel at sales.

Blind Trust

As you can see, the system is quite flawed and not likely to change.

Investing is no easy task on your own, so most people turn to a financial advisor. But they do that without the awareness that many of those same "advisors" may be better at destroying their wealth than at securing their future.

Yet, few people hold their advisors accountable for their investment performance. Why is this? A *Wall Street Journal* article asks that very question.[22] Interviewed for the article, Charles Rotblut of the American Association of Individual Investors says it may be something investors are simply not requesting. "I have to think investors would want to know that, but I don't know how many are actually asking for it," he said.

That's why you're very wise to be reading this guide and educating yourself. Many people listen to their advisors and simply trust that they have it all figured out. Some advisors, of course, are experienced experts who

---

[22] https://www.wsj.com/articles/financial-advisers-show-us-your-numbers-1405107222

can confidently navigate the markets. But many simply aren't—and while they may put on a brave face in front of clients, they might be as confused by the market as the average person likely is.

Now, the markets can be unpredictable, no doubt. However, if you study the financial markets, you can find market statistics that give you an edge. While I was employed to advise institutional clients, I read a landmark study by the Federal Reserve about signals that often predicted market imbalances that can lead to market downturns.[23] When I was working as a retail advisor, I talked with my colleagues about this research. Not one of them was aware of the landmark study. Not one.

So much for the cool professional who has studied and prepared for bear markets, bull markets, and everything in between.

Practice Makes Perfect

As an investor, however, you're unlikely to see your financial advisor sweat. Why? These Wall Street firms spend billions of dollars each year on marketing and sales training to create an illusion of confidence and control.

The financial advisor you sit across from has been interviewed or questioned dozens, if not hundreds of times

---

[23] Arturo Estrella and Gikas A. Hardouvelis, "The Term Predictor of Real Economic Activity," *The Journal of Finance* 46, no. 2 (June 1991), https://www.jstor.org/stable/2328836.

before. They have also likely been required to attend mandatory intensive training on how to gain your trust. Even the fresh-faced rookie who has just passed their regulatory exams has had dozens of hours of sales training designed to convince you of their professionalism, sincerity, integrity, and skill.

Consumers are at an incredible disadvantage. While these advisors deal with hundreds of investors, most people only have dealt with one or two advisors over their lifetime.

CHAPTER 4
Behind Wall Street's Facade

As you probably see, the reality is that many advisors are more skilled at managing their clients' emotions than managing their clients' money. But the fact is that the industry's stated purpose is the management of client wealth. So who is actually managing your money?

Meet the Models

When you initially hire a financial advisor, you often get an elaborate pitch about how they will tailor your investments to your specific needs. Well, that's not exactly how it works.

While some small independent advisors will do just that, it's not profitable for these giant Wall Street firms.

Instead, they develop "model portfolios."

So while the person sitting across from you says they are making investment decisions for you, they are probably putting you into whatever their research department recommended. Usually, that's based on one or more of the model portfolios.

Of course, there are probably many skilled people in their research department: real analysts. But here's the problem: these model portfolios are not tailored to you. They are tailored to the average person in your age range with your risk tolerance. But the average person probably doesn't have the same situation as you do. In fact, you might as well use random information, as two people the same age may have completely different financial situations.

So while they may provide the illusion that you're getting a customized experience, you probably aren't. You are probably in the same investments as most of their clients.

The Invisible Manager

Here's a secret that your Wall Street financial advisor will never tell you: when you invest with them, your money is managed by someone you never meet. And it's very likely the advisor doesn't meet or talk to them, either. Instead, your money is put into model portfolios and managed along with funds from millions of other investors by a few mutual fund managers. Needless to say, that's not quite the personal service they show on those slick TV commercials.

The net result is that your money may be invested incorrectly for your risk tolerance and goals. This can have negative consequences since you may be taking more risk than you want to or need to. This is often why people end up with significant drawdowns when the market turns south; they were invested more aggressively than they thought.

Who's Managing Risk?

This is the tragic part of Wall Street's "asset gatherer" mentality. Advisors are pressured to constantly add new clients, so the ball gets dropped when it comes to paying attention to your money. Often no one is managing your risk. So your life savings might just be a sitting duck out there. The market may have changed, but no one proactively makes necessary adjustments to your investments. Of course, the worst part of this is that the advisor is getting paid to professionally manage your money—but in reality, most are purely reactive and rarely focus on actively managing your risk.

Now, if you're 25 years old with no responsibilities, it may not matter. If your portfolio drops 40 percent in a bad year, it's not the end of the world.

But the reality is that many people experience dizzying

drops in their assets due to advisor incompetence or neglect. And it didn't have to happen.

Would You Like to Pay Twice?

Usually, the model portfolios are based on mutual funds or exchange-traded funds (ETFs). Mutual funds and ETFs have one very notable benefit: diversification. If you hold just a few stocks, and one gets hit with bad news or bad performance, it can cause you to lose a significant amount. With mutual funds or ETFs, you can spread that "company risk" across an entire sector or an entire index. Instead of owning a handful of companies, you own hundreds. So you spread out (and diversify away) much of that risk.

But here's the thing: if you have a financial advisor that puts your money into funds, did you know that you're paying two layers of management fees?

- First, you're paying your advisor a percentage of your assets every year.
- Second, you're also paying the mutual fund or ETF managers a percentage.

It is easy to miss since mutual fund and ETF managers take their fees directly out of the fund itself. So you'll never see the fees debited out of your money on your statement.

Your Alternatives

Is it worth it? In this case, your financial advisor's role is simply to pick mutual funds or ETFs for you, usually in the form of a model portfolio. Choosing these funds is not rocket science. Vanguard has built an entire subindustry around this premise—that investors can buy inexpensive index-linked mutual funds just fine and save a ton of money in the process. Or you could hire a financial planner for a few hours to help you decide which funds are best for your situation.

This move could save you potentially thousands of dollars per year and potentially hundreds of thousands of dollars over your investing career.

According to Moshe Milevsky, finance professor at York University's Schulich School of Business, if you invest $10,000 a year for 35 years and earn 5 percent a year, you will end up with $903,203. However, if you pay a 1 percent annual fee on that same investment, you'll only have $736,522. That small 1 percent annual fee has cost you over $166,000.

What About Other Services?

But there is more to securing your financial future than just investing. That's why the most valuable asset you can possibly have is a skilled financial advisor.

A high-quality financial advisor can provide you with

comprehensive financial planning. This process can help you create a strong foundation, avoid blind spots, and identify a clear path to achieve your goals. This also includes estate and tax planning to ensure you're not overpaying at tax time. Then retirement planning and asset protection planning can help you make sure that what you've built lasts.

And even more importantly, a quality advisor can help you prioritize your long-term financial goals amid your busy life. When the market gets rocky, they can be there to help you remember why you're invested the way you are. These advisors can be worth their weight in gold in those situations, saving investors from expensive mistakes.

So having a high-quality financial advisor can help you achieve your goals and feel more confident about your money. But as we've seen, it has to be the right one. But where to go to find the advisor you want?

Strangely, finding a good financial advisor has been made difficult by the industry. Wall Street prefers that you select a financial advisor based on their billion-dollar marketing. Financial media giants Barron's and CNBC annually publish financial advisor rankings, but before you place your faith in these rankings, you should know a couple of things.

Most importantly, the financial advisor's investment performance is not part of their ranking criteria. Barron's explains their reasoning in the fine print: "Investment returns are not a component of the rankings because an advisor's returns are dictated largely by the risk tolerance of clients." That's true, but it is also misleading. Risk tolerance is another term for "investment policy" or "investment benchmark."

A mutual fund's returns are also largely dictated by their published investment policy or investment benchmark. What prudent investor chooses a mutual fund without being concerned if it outperforms their stated benchmark? Further, financial advisors can have their investment performance verified just as a mutual fund does. More on that later.

The second thing investors need to know about the Barron's and CNBC rankings is that they provide an income stream to these media companies. Financial advisor firms may choose to pay money to advertise their inclusion on the list, though it must be noted that it costs nothing to submit the application to be considered.

How do Barron's and CNBC make money off their rankings? When a firm is ranked highly, they use the "news" to market their services—being highly ranked by a national media organization is good for business.

But to advertise their ranking the financial firms must pay a licensing fee. The fine print from one such firm, who will remain anonymous, reads, "Firm XYZ has not paid a fee to participate in the rankings but has paid fees for a license to access reprints and distribute links to the results of the rankings via email, social media, and the firm's website for a prescribed period of time."

The top financial advisor firms eagerly pay to license and publish their Barron's or CNBC ranking to attract new clients or to solidify their relationship with existing clients but will not spend money to have their investment performance verified.

The rankings themselves raise some eyebrows to those in the industry. When Barron's began ranking financial advisors, generally the advisors ranked higher had more assets under management than lower ranked advisors. Since the amount of assets a financial advisor manages generally dictates the level of the firm's revenues, it is easy to make a disturbing connection. If you were responsible for generating marketing revenues at Barron's, would you rather be licensing to larger firms, with larger revenues, or smaller firms, with smaller revenues? After you consider their ranking criteria and the financial media's marketing revenue model, it's reasonable to be wary of these rankings.

CHAPTER 5

Misconduct—Misconduct Everywhere

In Chapter 6, I outline specific strategies so you can find a high-quality, skilled advisor. But first, let's look at how we got here. Clearly, this situation is highly unfavorable to investors. But at the same time, this industry claims to benefit investors.

How exactly did we get here—where did all of this start?

The Evolution of a Monster

As we previously covered, most wealth management firms don't require investment knowledge or experience to get hired—only passing the regulatory exam. Additionally, most firms don't really encourage their advisors to brush up on their investing skills.

These lax standards are the result of an evolution that started with the dot-com bubble of the late 1990s. At that time, it was not uncommon for advisors to charge 2 to 3 percent in management fees per year to investors. With that level of revenue, advisors could earn a good living serving a small group of clients.

But that was before extreme greed took hold of both Wall Street and Main Street. In the late 1990s, technology stocks were booming. It was not uncommon for a tech stock to jump double digits in a week. And since the internet and cable television now brought news to us 24/7, everyone saw the riches multiply. The topic of every conversation at every party? Stocks!

And it wasn't just the young and tech-savvy, either. All ages wanted in.

Many financial advisors were trying to fight the trend, warning people that it could be a bubble. But as tech stocks skyrocketed persisted, most financial advisors surrendered and started putting pretty much everyone, including retirees, into technology stocks—primarily because the clients demanded it.

Of course, Wall Street firms were in on it too—stoking the fires of greed. Their analysts were slapping buy recommendations on stocks with no profits and little earnings. For Merrill Lynch, this turned into a $100 million lesson when they were later taken to court by then New York Attorney General Eliot Spitzer. Internal emails showed that while Merrill analysts rated these dot-com companies publicly as "buy" or "strong buy," those same analysts privately referred to them as "pieces of junk."[24]

Once the music stopped, many of these stocks fell precipitously. Even high-quality technology stocks like Cisco Systems would lose over 60 percent of their value. Those who held Cisco were lucky, as many of the speculative internet stocks quickly collapsed 90 percent or more. Many companies declared bankruptcy and went out of business.

Billions of dollars of investor money were wiped out. MarketWatch characterized the end of the dot-com bust this way: "The bust ended a brief but phenomenally lucrative period for investors willing to take a chance on unproven technology companies…and on largely unproven fund managers who claimed to understand them."[25]

Lawsuits Galore

Out of the ashes came lawsuits—thousands of lawsuits

---

[24] Maria Teresa Cometto, "Market Shaken by Merrill Lynch Investigation," IPE, June 2002, https://www.ipe.com/market-shaken-by-merrill-lynch-investigation/15174.article.

[25] Jonathan Burton, "Former Internet-Fund Stars 10 Years After the Bust," MarketWatch, March 8, 2010, https://www.marketwatch.com/story/former-internet-fund-stars-10-years-after-the-bust-2010-03-08.

asking for billions of dollars in damages from Wall Street firms. Many alleged that financial advisors should have known and prevented unsophisticated investors from taking on the risks associated with firms with no track record. To be fair, many of these plaintiffs had invested in stocks that their financial advisors warned them against. But greed is a hard thing to overcome.

Big Wall Street firms and their lawyers saw the writing on the wall. They knew they would get hauled into courts all across America. Juries would see the Wall Street executives and their expensive legal team sitting across from somebody's grandmother who had lost half her retirement savings. Wall Street did not stand a chance.

This was not a risk they were willing to take. So the Wall Street behemoths settled with thousands of plaintiffs, avoiding lengthy and embarrassing courtroom trials. Merrill Lynch alone settled with state and federal regulators for the sum of $100 million. The events that transpired changed the financial industry.

A New Day and a New Way

After that debacle, the lawyers took control of Wall Street. That was no surprise, since they were still paying out to investors that had lost a lot of money.

At the same time, regulators were now looking over their shoulders, wondering how analysts could be recommending stocks to the investing public while privately calling them bad investments. The truth was that the analysts were pressured to provide rosy ratings for corporations so the investment banking side of the firm could win lucrative investment banking business.

Henry Blodget was one of the analysts that the public looked to when deciding on a company's future prospects. Institutional Investor interviewed him in 2020 about his role in the bursting of the dot-com bubble and his buy ratings on stocks that were hard to justify.

> *In one case, Blodget gave digital company GoTo.com a satisfactory rating in a 2001 Merrill report, saying investors should hold on to its shares. But the SEC singled out his GoTo.com rating as an example of fraud: When the regulator combed through Blodget's emails, it found that after an institutional client had asked, "What's so interesting about GoTo except banking fees????," Blodget had replied, "Nothing."*[26]

The list of Wall Street wrongdoings was long, and the public scrutiny was not letting up. Amid all this craziness, the lawyers moved in to do damage control.

---

[26] Michelle Celarier, "Henry Blodget Was Banned From the Financial Industry. So He Built a Financial Media Empire. Business Insider's Happy Warrior Fights to the End," Institutional Investor, July 28, 2020, https://www.institutionalinvestor.com/article/b1mpnkdvcmpcp9/Henry-Blodget-Was-Banned-From-the-Financial-Industry-So-He-Built-a-Financial-Media-Empire.

Meet the Investor Risk Questionnaire

Wall Street and its army of high-priced lawyers needed to find a way to insulate the wealth management business from future liability. So they went back to their law books and concocted a new strategy to avoid liability for inappropriate risk-taking. And Penn & Teller would have been proud! They would change the focus of the wealth management business to *asset allocation*.

Asset allocation is an investment strategy that aims to balance risk and reward by apportioning a portfolio's assets according to an individual's goals. In more practical terms, it is a framework outlining how much risk each investor wants to take. While this was not a new concept, the lawyers came up with a key new step in the process. Going forward, the advisor would put the asset allocation plan in writing and get the customer to sign it.

Asset Allocation's Rise to Fame

To avoid raising eyebrows, they needed a way to sell this new plan. So the Wall Street's marketing machine unearthed a paper written in 1986 that concluded that asset allocation determines 90 percent of a portfolio's volatility.[27]

---

[27] Gary P. Brinson, L. Randolph Hood, Gilbert L. Beebower, "Determinants of Portfolio Performance," *Financial Analysts Journal* 42, no. 4 (July-August, 1986): 39-44, https://www.jstor.org/stable/4478947.

However, the masters of disguise spun it slightly differently. They started telling investors that asset allocation is responsible for 90 percent of a portfolio's performance. This altered interpretation spread like wildfire and was used to promote the value of this new process to customers.

Does repeating a rumor make it true? Allan Roth at CBS News Moneywatch put it this way:

> *There is an often (really often) repeated statement that "90% of your return can be explained by your asset allocation." It's just not true, and the frequency with which it is repeated isn't making it any truer.*[28]

Regardless, the plan was masterful, as the concept really took hold in an industry always on the lookout to avoid accountability. Today, you will not find a client agreement that does not include an asset allocation model that must approved in writing. It is standard operating procedure for the industry. So began the rise of the Investor Risk Questionnaire. Now you'll find these at every wealth management firm in the country, without exception. The questionnaires do vary in length and detail, but typically ask similar key questions:

---

[28] Allan Roth, "A Misconception—90 Percent of Return Comes from Asset Allocation," CBS News, December 20, 2009, https://www.cbsnews.com/news/a-misconception-90-percent-of-return-comes-from-asset-allocation/.

- What's your time horizon? This is asked in plain English because they really want to know when you might ask for your money back.

- What's your target return? Here they want to know about how much you expect to earn on your money each year.

- What's your comfort level with big losses? They'll ask how much you're prepared to lose on paper until you scream "uncle."

Do the questionnaires help? Research shows that in many cases, your risk tolerance may change with the market.[29] That's not hard to understand, as everyone is happy to take more risk when the market's soaring. But once the market corrects, fear reigns and the average person becomes cautious again.

Regardless, these questionnaires are still widely in use. While the exact terminology used may be different, these are the types of questions you can expect. The key? Getting your signature on this document. If you ever decided to sue, the firm will pull out this form to prove that you knew you were taking on the risk of loss.

---

[29] Rebecca Lake, "How Risk Tolerance Questionnaires Can Steer You Wrong," *U.S. News & World Report*, July 25, 2017, https://money.usnews.com/investing/articles/2017-07-25/how-risk-tolerance-questionnaires-can-steer-you-wrong.

Multipurpose Tool

Once you fill out the questionnaire, your answers are put into a computer and out pops a spiffy "asset allocation model." These details will again vary by firm, but most have one thing in common: they provide a specific template for your portfolio, all driven by your wishes.

The asset allocation model will set forth the percentages you will hold in stocks and in bonds. In some cases, it may provide further detail to show your appropriate allocation to individual categories of stocks and bonds (such as small-cap versus large-cap stocks or growth versus value).

Then, that same questionnaire will typically be provided for your review annually.

Does It Work?

Was this new procedure the smashing success that Wall Street built it up to be? Did customer investment results suddenly take a quantum leap forward once Wall Street saw the asset allocation light? Since you've read this far, you probably already know the answer.

While it may incidentally help you get a more appropriate portfolio, the real reason it exists is to insulate the firm from liability. Fortunately, there are a few positive by-products of this process. For one, this documented asset allocation model can help the wealth management's compliance department detect improper trades early before one isolated trade grows into a damaging pattern.

But this system also effectively ties the hands of the financial advisor. That was by design.

Who Is Advising Who?

There's another result of Wall Street's damage control, and that's the centralization of investment advice. They could no longer afford to have their advisors free to recommend investments to clients—that didn't turn out too well during the dot-com crash. Instead, they made another significant change to their business model.

These individuals still provide financial advice, but now it's not usually theirs. The advice they give you about investing is now mostly generated far, far away, at the corporate Mother Ship. There, number-crunching analysts create those model portfolios that are then passed on to individual advisors.

Most people think their advisor conducts research, then carefully structures each client's portfolio based on their goals and needs. While they may work hard to create that illusion, it's far likelier that your money is simply put into a model portfolio that matches your client risk questionnaire. And equally as likely that your portfolio looks a whole lot like all of the other clients at the firm.

Good for Business

While this is great for the firm, it's not usually good for you. You are led to think you're getting tailored advice, but you're not. And here's the biggest problem for you: no one is focused on managing risks specific to your situation. But let's not forget this system was put in place to manage the firm's risks—not yours.

Along with reducing risk, there is another significant benefit to the wealth management firm in adopting this process. Mutual fund firms pay to get onto the "supermarket shelf" of these big wealth management firms. You don't think that they're going to just let any mutual fund be suggested by their financial advisors, do you? The highest bidder usually wins.

These firms are in it to make money, and if the client happens to make money too, that's an unexpected bonus. There's very little disclosure about these arrangements between mutual funds and wealth management firms, so most people are not even aware they exist. But these hidden arrangements often determine what ends up in your account.

And unfortunately, it is usually the investor that ends up funding the kickback that the mutual fund pays to the firm. It is a cost of doing business, so usually that expense just gets factored into the fund fees. You're probably seeing a pattern here: in the wealth management business, everyone gets paid. Retail investors end up at the bottom of the food chain, so they end up paying the price. However, the tracks are covered so you never see this expense. But that doesn't make it any less real to your bottom line.

Fortunately, the mutual funds suggested by the firms usually have some positive aspects to them to make the sale easier. In this regard, the venerable firm Morningstar plays a key role, assigning rankings, or stars, to mutual funds. And in recent years, many advisors have directed their clients to exchange-traded funds (ETFs) to save on management fees.

However, it is likely that with a genuinely objective advisor, or even on your own, you could find a similar fund or ETF for far less than you are paying. And remember, as covered previously, if your advisor simply puts you in mutual funds, you are paying for two layers of financial management. Now, this might be worth it if you're getting other services such as tax and estate planning. But bottom line, you need to know what you are paying because Wall Street will not tell you.

The Annual Review

Another strategy the lawyers recommended was the creation of more standardized processes. This would help them keep those individual advisors under control, to again help minimize liability. One area that was standardized was the annual review.

The purpose of the annual review should be for you to evaluate your advisor, right? Normally, reviews provide a chance for those paying for the service to review the provider.

Wall Street, however, had other ideas. Instead of you reviewing your advisor and their investment performances, they decided to flip things around. So who produces the annual review report? The advisor! Imagine if employees, rather than their employer, could create their own performance review! In the Wall Street world of illusions, it's just another carefully strategized move.

So, of course, many advisors do whatever it takes to make that report card look as favorable as possible. One popular tactic is improper benchmarking.

Benchmarking is a term for comparison. When you are paying someone a percentage of your assets every year to manage your investments, it's important to have something to compare to. Normally, you'll use a bond index, along with the S&P 500 or a global stock index. Here's the problem: your asset allocation model is probably not allocated like the benchmarks your portfolio is getting compared to. This is a no-no that would never fly in the institutional world, but very, very few retail investors have enough technical knowledge to recognize this.

Ideally, during positive years, you want a financial advisor who can help you match or exceed market gains while taking less risk than your asset allocation model. At the same time, that advisor should be taking defensive actions to help you lose less when the market drops.

Or if you're more aggressive, you may just want your financial advisor to beat the market's returns without regard to the amount of risk required. But taking more risk means you'll probably incur bigger losses at times, too. Remember that it's not just about returns—it's about the amount of risk taken to achieve those returns.

Bottom line, your advisor should do better for you than the market on a risk/return basis, after their fees are accounted for. Because if they can't, your retirement account would be better off in an index fund for a fraction of the cost.

Since that strategy is a real danger to Wall Street revenues, the lawyers came up with a tactic: minimize focus on the benchmarks altogether. Today, benchmarking is not even required by regulators.[30] Many advisors are happy to keep it that way, as it saves them many uncomfortable conversations.

But if financial advisors aren't willing to be held accountable for their investing advice, why are they charging you a percentage of your investments every year? Wouldn't an hourly fee or flat financial planning fee be far more appropriate? I believe so.

In an ideal world, every financial advisor's performance

---

[30] David J. Drucker, "The Case Against Benchmarking," *Financial Advisor Magazine*, August 2005, https://www.fa-mag.com/news/article-1190.html?issue=59.

should also be reviewed by an independent, expert third party. In today's automated world, that is possible, and I talk about that in Chapter 6.

Arbitration Nation

Even with all these changes, the lawyers weren't done yet. There were other damage control measures implemented after the disastrous dot-com fallout. One thing they knew for sure: they wanted to keep their wealth management staff out of court. They needed more control. So their next step was to include mandatory arbitration clauses in all client contracts.

The financial industry self-regulation organization, FINRA, offers a mandatory arbitration program. Most wealth management contracts require the use of that system in their client contracts.

At first glance, that can sound like a benefit for consumers. Years ago, arbitration had a glowing reputation. Faster than courts and dramatically less expensive, it was billed as a great advancement for everyday folks, helping to ensure a fair shake.

However, since that time, arbitration has evolved. And lawyers have figured out that they needed to join the system or lose business, so now you'll often pay similar attorney fees for either one.

While it still can be faster than court, sometimes arbitration can be even slower. Plus, you also have to pay your share of the arbitrators' fees. And there are usually three of them. The judge is on a salary in court, so it doesn't cost you extra after court fees.

But here's what is important: an arbitrator is not a judge. They don't have anyone looking over their shoulder as judges do in court, where their actions are subject to public scrutiny. There's little screening to make sure the arbitrators have the mindset and experience to be objective and fair.

Even if an arbitrator likes the idea of being fair, human nature often wins over. This may lead to them giving more favorable rulings to firms since they are repeat arbitration users. By gaining favor with firms, they may help improve their odds of more assignments.

Individuals, on the other hand, usually use this system only once. As much as the arbitrator may want to rule in your favor, you're not likely to help them get more work in the future. And favoring the consumer might be a quick way to end their lucrative part-time career as an arbitrator.

Of course, there are probably many arbitrators that are committed to being fair to consumers. However, there are probably not enough, because in 2014, *USA Today* reported on a study that concluded that FINRA arbitrations were unfair to investors. Among the findings of the research:

- 80 percent of the arbitrators were male.
- The average age of an arbitrator was 69, much older than the average investor filing a claim.

- The selection process did not focus on choosing impartial arbitrators, and information on arbitrators' backgrounds was not kept up to date.

- Investors were awarded damages in less than half the cases decided from 2009 to 2014.[31]

Jason Doss, an Atlanta attorney and president of the Public Investors Arbitration Bar Association (PIABA), the group that conducted the analysis, notes that "PIABA has shown that FINRA's arbitrator disclosure process fails at every step," adding, "investors have no other choice but to conclude that arbitration is unfair."[32]

Arbitration is also binding, meaning that unless fraud is found and can be proved, there is no appeal. The arbitrator panel's decision is final. And if that decision has to do with your life savings, the impact on your future can be far-reaching.

Good Luck Collecting

Let's say you are one of the lucky ones and win your case in arbitration. You may now have another problem: collecting your damages.

Even though you have to pay a $1,400 fee to file a

---

[31] Kevin McCoy, "Report: Arbitrations May Be Unfair to Investors," *USA Today*, October 7, 2014, https://www.usatoday.com/story/money/business/2014/10/07/finra-arbitration-pool-flaws/16855769/.

[32] Ibid.

claim, FINRA is clear on its website that it will not help you collect any award you receive:

"FINRA's arbitration forum does not ensure payment of damages awarded."[33]

According to FINRA data from December 2020, over 22 percent of awards from 2015 were still not paid five years later. Many of these unpaid awards are not small amounts either—the median award left unpaid after five years was $245,200. The highest outstanding award from five years ago was over $4.5 million. And as you might expect, an even higher percentage of more recent awards remained unpaid.[34]

FINRA has begun taking action against delinquent advisors and firms by initiating suspension procedures. The problem is that many of these advisors who owe money have left the industry, so FINRA has lost its leverage against them. In that case, investors are forced to go to court to attempt to collect these amounts. This process often involves chasing an individual through bankruptcy court, which is another gamble since there's no guarantee that anything will be left to collect.

---

[33] "Statistics on Unpaid Customer Awards in FINRA Arbitration," FINRA, accessed March 11, 2022, https://www.finra.org/arbitration-mediation/statistics-unpaid-customer-awards-finra-arbitration.

[34] Ibid.

Accredited for What?

If you've got more resources, the situation can get even more complicated. In some cases, your assets or income may automatically categorize you as an "accredited investor."

The wealth management firm helping you will make a big deal of this and make sure you're flattered, and of course it does indicate you've been successful. This gains you other privileges too—there are some investments that only accredited investors can gain access to.

Sounds great, right? Unfortunately, this simple categorization can be turned against you. In fact, Wall Street advisors love it: they can sell you many different investment products, most of which pay much higher commissions. But the unfortunate fact is that while you may have a high income or high net worth, your expertise is probably not investing. You probably still rely on your financial advisor for advice.

However, in the eyes of FINRA, you may still be deemed financially sophisticated simply because of your net worth or income. When these cases go to arbitration, the firms and arbitrators will frequently take the position that "you should have known" as a sophisticated investor. In reality, this opaque industry does everything in its power to hide the truth from its clients. The only people who usually understand these complex regulations are those who work in the wealth management industry. Or as Penn & Teller might say, those who have seen behind the curtain.

The Fox in the Hen House?

Speaking of the regulators, where are they in this whole mess? Surely, they are actively working to protect investors from all these issues, right? In this case, FINRA is, in theory, the premiere organization in charge of regulating the financial advisory industry. But it is a unique animal: instead of a government entity, FINRA is a "self-regulatory" organization.

Yes, it's about as fishy as it sounds.

InvestmentNews calls FINRA "the watchdog no one is watching."[35] They go on to say, "FINRA writes its own rules, meets behind closed doors and releases information if and when it deems necessary."

Securities industry attorney Alan Wolper wrote an article entitled "How Do You Make a Million Dollars? Become Part of FINRA Senior Management!" This article highlights the fact that FINRA executives are paid exorbitant salaries for mostly part-time work.[36]

---

[35] Mark Schoeff Jr. and Bruce Kelly, "FINRA: Who's Watching the Watchdog?" InvestmentNews, September 2, 2017, https://www.investmentnews.com/finra-whos-watching-the-watchdog-72102.

[36] Alan Wolper, "How Do You Make a Million Dollars? Become Part of FINRA Senior Management!" Ulmer Attorneys, July 2, 2015, https://www.bdlawcorner.com/2015/07/how-do-you-make-a-million-dollars-become-part-of-finra-senior-management/.

Consumer groups have also highlighted that FINRA's BrokerCheck program, designed for investor protection, is flawed and missing much information available from state regulators. After repeatedly informing FINRA of these numerous omissions, FINRA did nothing and continues to market BrokerCheck as a "complete resource."[37] The groups requested that FINRA add this missing data, or at least put a disclaimer on the site that recommends consumers contact their state regulator. To date, these omissions have not been corrected, and no obvious disclaimer has been added.

Further, remember the issue of FINRA not being particularly helpful to consumers to collect delinquent arbitration awards? Believe it or not, it was far worse previously. So bad that, in 2018, there was a bipartisan bill sponsored by a Democrat and a Republican to require FINRA to set up a relief fund to repay consumers with unpaid arbitration awards.

Republican senator John Kennedy of Louisiana said of this bill: "These investors have already been swindled out of their money once, and thousands of them still haven't been given their unpaid arbitration. Our bill aims to fix

---

[37] Hugh D. Berkson and Marnie C. Lambert, "BrokerCheck—The Inequality of Investor Access to Information Remains Unabated—An Update to PIABA's March 2014 Report," accessed March 11, 2022, https://piaba.org/sites/default/files/newsroom/2016-10/Broker%20Check%20Update%20(October%2020,%202016).pdf.

that."[38]

Not surprisingly, the bill was hotly contested by industry members. Ultimately, it failed.

So, unfortunately, FINRA is not the investor protection agency that it is cracked up to be.

Caveat Emptor

As you can see, the deck is unfortunately firmly stacked against individual investors. Now that you know that, let's move on to a much more important subject: what can you do to get the advice you need while keeping your money safe?

---

[38] Tracey Longo, "Republican Joins Elizabeth Warren to Force FINRA to Pay For Deadbeat Brokers," FinancialAdvisor, May 31, 2018, https://www.fa-mag.com/news/republican-joins-elizabeth-warren-to-force-finra-to-pay-for-deadbeat-brokers-38964.html.

CHAPTER 6
How to Protect Your Money and Your Future

The burnt customer certainly prefers to believe that he has been robbed rather than that he has been a fool on the advice of fools.

—Fred Schwed Jr.,
Where Are the Customers' Yachts[39]

My hope for this guide was to educate you on the inner workings of this industry so you can be aware of the sleight of hand that you may experience when working with a financial advisor.

---

[39] Fred Schwed Jr., *Where Are the Customers' Yachts? Or a Good Look at Wall Street* (Hoboken: Wiley, 2006).

Thankfully, most financial advisors are good people. The vast majority, I believe, mean well, but the Wall Street business model doesn't support or motivate them to serve their clients as their clients might be led to believe. That aside, I'm seeing more independent advisors taking a stand against these practices and helping individuals navigate this minefield.

According to a 2022 study by Cerulli, the total population of financial advisors will fall by 2025—however, independent advisors will actually increase their numbers.[40]

The fact remains: a skilled, objective, and ethical financial advisor can be the key to securing your future and achieving your goals. So in this final chapter, I'll give you a step-by-step plan to help you find those real advisors who are capable of managing your money effectively.

Step 1: Insist on a Fiduciary

First things first: when you pay someone money to provide you a service—any service—they should be required to put your interests first. Period. So always ask if the financial advisor agrees to act as your fiduciary. If they say yes, ask them to put it in writing, and keep that

---

[40] Lynnley Browning, "6 Major Trends for Financial Advisors in 2022: Cerulli Study," February 21, 2022, https://www.financial-planning.com/list/financial-advisors-from-brokerages-to-independent-firms-are-in-for-stark-changes-according-to-a-cerulli-study.

document in a safe place.

If a prospective (or current) financial advisor is not willing to act as your fiduciary or hesitates to put that writing, run—don't walk—away. You need someone who provides real advice.

Step 2: Ask About Potential Conflicts of Interest

Second, while working with a fiduciary is a start, other hidden conflicts of interest may exist. Again, take a trick from the Wall Street playbook and ask them to spell out any potential conflicts of interest that exist with their service in simple terms. Ask for that in writing.

They likely have that all documented in fine print in their contract somewhere, but you want them to walk you through it all in plain English.

A high-quality, ethical advisor will completely understand and respect that you are educated enough to ask this question so will have no problem doing this for you. Plus, there will be little or nothing to disclose.

Any hesitation or unwillingness is a valuable warning to walk away and keep looking.

Step 3: Check Their Regulatory Record

Third, you should check out any potential advisor's regulatory record. Look for any red flags, such as arbitrations or disciplinary actions.

You can check out their FINRA record at https://brokercheck.finra.org/.

It is also prudent to contact your state regulator since consumer groups have flagged the FINRA records as often being incomplete.[41]

And one practical note on reviewing regulatory records: a regulatory infraction or two should not disqualify a financial advisor completely from consideration. Sometimes the client was in the wrong, but the firm demanded the financial advisor settle and take the punishment, thereby harming the advisor but keeping the firm's name out of the newspapers.

But obviously, reviewing everything and asking questions is critical.

With these three steps, you have now narrowed your potential choices down to those with ethics who are free of significant conflicts of interest.

But even the most ethical advisor, while well-intentioned, is not enough. Are they good at their jobs? Are they good investors? If they're not, they can still be hazardous to your wealth.

So, you're not done yet.

---

[41] Janet Kidd Stewart, "Critics Find BrokerCheck Background Checks Incomplete," *Chicago Tribune*, June 6, 2015, https://www.chicagotribune.com/business/success/sc-cons-0611-journey-20150606-column.html.

Step 4: Ask About Their Investing Edge

Your financial advisor can add value to your investment portfolio in a few ways:

1. Security selection: they can carefully screen and choose investments that offer a better risk/return profile than the agreed-to benchmark.
2. They can also "time the market" so that you can buy and sell at better price points (buy low and sell high).
3. They might incorporate other strategies like selling options to increase income from your existing positions.
4. Finally, some improved performance can also be gained by incorporating tax strategies to keep more of what you earn.

Advisors may use one or a combination of these strategies—

Security selection is a common strategy. Several mutual fund managers reached the zenith of their careers through the careful selection of securities to include in their portfolio—Peter Lynch, John Templeton, and Dana Emery, to name a few.

As for market timing, there's widespread consensus that the most successful hedge fund of all time is the Renaissance Technologies' Medallion fund. It gave investors an annualized return of almost 40 percent after fees. The Medallion fund was created and managed by non-financial scientists and mathematicians. It's a safe bet to say their returns had virtually nothing to do with traditional security analysis.

Many Wall Street and financial advisor marketing materials reference academic studies that claim that market timing does not work. But the reality is that some people can time the markets and have done so consistently over more extended periods. The key is that these firms usually have a disciplined and repeatable system that works the majority of the time. As importantly, they typically have a similar system in place to cut losses quickly.

The key is that if your advisor has some type of edge, they should be able to describe it to you clearly and back it up with actual results.

One caveat: some advisors may have their hands tied when it comes to specific account types. For example, most people have a qualified retirement account that enjoys tax advantages (such as a 401[k] or an IRA). Calculating portfolio returns is easier since taxes are not part of the equation in these accounts.

When it comes to your taxable accounts, calculating returns becomes a bit more complex because tax strategies come into play. Of course, that presents a potential opportunity that some advisors will use to help you gain better after-tax results.

What's the point of all this? Ask your financial advisor what their edge is. Why should you allow them to manage your funds if their investing skill cannot beat less expensive index funds? Ask them directly, "Is your investment edge in security selection or timing the market? Or something else?"

Then track their performance as the institutional money managers do. We'll go how to do that in the next and final step.

Step 5: Most Importantly, Assess Their Investing Skills

Wall Street does everything in its power to avoid you asking about your financial advisor's investment skills. But when it comes to managing your money, could there be a more important question? After all, you need someone to help you safely grow wealth, not make it disappear.

Just like if you are looking for a surgeon for critical surgery, you need to know how often the surgeries have positive outcomes. Or would you just ignore their results and be happy with just any surgeon? Or if you hire a lawyer, you'd ask about their record in court. Do they usually win?

Yet, if you ask a financial advisor for proof that they are a skilled investor, few—very few—will produce a documented record for you. What they will produce in its place is what sounds like a perfectly legitimate excuse why they can't provide a documented track record.

Even the industry's regulator, FINRA, tries to guide investors away from the topic of investment performance. To illustrate that point, the following text has previously appeared on the FINRA website:

> *Be cautious of any investment professional who promises you above-average account performance or says you'll be making risk-free investments. Nobody can guarantee that your investments will grow at a particular rate or that you won't lose money.*[42]

And contained in every mutual fund advertisement are the words, "past performance is not indicative of future results." Of course, there are no guarantees, and there is always risk with investments. No one can tell you exactly how much you'll earn each year. And part of properly evaluating performance is assessing how much risk is taken to generate those returns. However, shouldn't a professional be better at managing that risk than individuals who don't do this for a living? Shouldn't they be more disciplined at protecting capital?

Can you imagine hiring anyone for anything important without wanting to look at their performance? If you build a house, don't you consider the builder's past results? Suppose some of the houses were discovered as

---

[42] Matt Koppenheffer, "How to Assess Your Financial Advisor's Performance," The Motley Fool, April 7, 2017, https://www.fool.com/investing/general/2012/05/11/how-to-assess-your-financial-advisors-performance.aspx.

faulty after a few years or couldn't withstand a few rainstorms because the builder didn't think to prepare for those. Would you dismiss that as irrelevant?

Of course, we all know that no one has a crystal ball. But bottom line, you have nothing else to guide your decision except the sales skill of the person trying to get hired by you.

So this step is a little trickier, but there are things you can do.

Look for an Independently Verified Track Record (GIPS®)

First, you can look for a financial advisor that provides an independently verified track record of their investment performance. However, given today's sales-oriented Wall Street business model, they are not easy to find, and the financial media completely ignores financial advisor investment performance as we have seen with the Barron's and CNBC financial advisor rankings. Protecting your wealth really is up to you.

I suggest you email some local financial advisory firms and ask them if they provide a Global Investment Performance Standards (GIPS®) compliant performance report. GIPS® is a worldwide set of investment reporting standards maintained by the nonprofit Chartered Financial Analyst Institute. It is accepted globally as a gold standard for investment professionals to follow.

Once you find a few GIPS® compliant firms, interview

them and take the time to do some real due diligence—just like the institutions do. Verify their past employment, check their academic and regulatory licensing records. If the firm is a small one, you can even ask the firm to provide you with credit reports on the firm's principals. Last, contact the auditing group that produced the investment performance report and confirm the figures.

What if you have an advisor you like or can't find a GIPS® compliant advisor?

What About Non-GIPS® Performance Reporting?

Remember when I talked about financial advisors producing their own performance reporting and what a conflict of interest that is? Not to mention the overwhelming majority of performance reports don't tell you if your investment portfolio is being skillfully managed. They do not provide you with the answer to the question, "Is my financial advisor's investment skill worth the fees I pay?" If your investment portfolio is being skillfully managed, you should be earning returns superior to that of your asset allocation model but with less risk.

So how can you conclusively know if your portfolio benefits from your financial advisor's investment skill or if the fees you pay only act as a drag on your portfolio's performance?

It's the question I'm aiming to answer. I've assembled a team, and we are rolling out a new service:

FinancialAdvisorCheck.com. This service produces a third-party performance report on your investment portfolio without the knowledge of your investment advisor. The report is created for you and is never shared with anyone else. In this regard, FinancialAdvisorCheck.com acts like your own personal consultant. Our goal is to become the sole source for portfolio performance reporting in much the same way Morningstar is for mutual fund performance reporting.

In addition to providing you the information you need to assess your advisor's performance, the service will, in the future, also aggregate the investment performance of all the advisors tracked so you can see how your advisor stacks up against their peers.

This report is created using the same approach and algorithms that large institutions use. But the key is that FinancialAdvisorCheck.com is independent of any Wall Street financial institution. The firm is 100 percent independently owned and operated and receives no revenues, value, or anything else from anyone other than clients. Our allegiance is only to you, the investor, to help you escape the tentacles of salespeople masquerading as skilled financial advisors.

The best part? It's 100 percent free to the first 10,000 users that sign up and help contribute to the service's development.

Why are we offering you a free service? Because we want to clean up the industry so that no family ever feels the level of financial stress that led to my brother's suicide.

There is another part to this, though. Over the past few decades, financial advisory fees have been cratering. This fee compression acts as a type of competitive advantage to financial advisors that are, in reality, salespeople. Salespeople can use lower fees to attract business away from financial advisors skilled in investment management.

The industry encourages it. Robo advisors and national advisory firms routinely champion their fee structure rather than their investment performance record.

FinancialAdvisorCheck.com wants skilled financial advisors to be recognized and we hope to help reverse the fee slide that often discourages skilled financial advisors. Lastly, we want salespeople masquerading as financial advisors to be identified.

What About Discount Brokers and Advisor Matching Services?

Last, I know many investors simply avoid the hassle and use a discount broker. That's fine, but please be aware that the people you speak with on the phone are frequently not fiduciaries. They have not come to know you, your family, or your circumstances.

Finally, I get lots of questions concerning online

services that claim to pair you with a vetted financial advisor. All of the services I have seen that do this are pay-to-play. That means that the advisor signs up and then pays for the opportunity to be "paired" with you. So, unfortunately, that should tell you all you need to know.

Your Next Steps

By now, you probably see that there's more to getting the right financial advice than just hiring your friend's advisor. Unfortunately, most people don't know what to ask and simply hire someone they like or someone their friend or family recommends. Given the potential impact on your future, you can't afford to take shortcuts.

So please refer to this book when you research and interview advisors to make sure you only consider those who deserve your business.

Interested in learning more about the technical side of investment reporting? I've included an appendix at the end of this book that provides a deeper dive. That material can help you understand more details about properly evaluating your advisor.

Also, make use of our free offer to receive our independent investment performance reporting on your current advisor. For now, there's no cost or risk to you, and it might just help you avoid many of the illusions (and nightmares) covered in this book.

Get a Free Financial Advisor Check: About FinancialAdvisorCheck.com

FinancialAdvisorCheck.com helps investors monitor their financial advisor's investment performance. Our unique service uses institutional grade, bank-level security to provide you with an independent report detailing your advisors' investment performance results. Learn more about us at financialadvisorcheck.com.

Questions or comments?
Email us at info@financialadvisorcheck.com

APPENDIX
A Deeper Dive Into Investment Reporting

I'm glad you're still reading! It's smart to be informed. In this section, we'll get into more detail on investment portfolio reporting.

Let's look at the differences between the investment portfolio reporting given to individuals versus institutions. As I mentioned earlier, institutional investors demand thorough, standardized reporting verified or prepared by an independent third party. Sadly, retail investors usually receive the opposite.

Conflicts of Interest

The first and the single most crucial difference is one we have already covered: conflicts of interest. Never, and I mean never, allow a financial advisor to produce a review of their own work product. That is such a blatant conflict of interest that common sense tells you that it should be outlawed. But sadly, the regulatory agencies are in Wall Street's pocket.

Common Aspects of Retail Reviews and Reporting

Investment reporting to the retail investor most commonly takes the form of "annual reviews." These reviews usually start with a few basics:

1. Formal account name
2. Financial advisor name
3. List of assets held and amounts
4. Investment return for your portfolio for the previous year, and usually since inception
5. Some benchmark indexes to compare it against, such as the S&P 500 and bond or T-Bill indexes

Relative Performance

Relative Performance

	Avg. Annual Retuen	Standard Deviation	Portfolio Value
Portfolio	6.3%	6.8%	$864,776
Stock Index	8.6%	16.2%	$965,175
US Bond Market Index	4.6%	3.5%	$748,998
US Treasury Bill 30 Days	0.49%	0.5%	$504,889

The Asset Allocation Model

Next, these reports will usually show your "custom" asset allocation model. This is your portfolio's benchmark. Each asset category has been selected for its risk and return characteristics. The amount assigned to each asset class is the result of a custom algorithm created by your financial advisor's firm. The answers you provided about your investment time horizon, return goals, and "pain threshold" regarding market downturns were all input into the algorithm.

At some earlier point in time, you and your financial advisor likely reviewed and agreed to the asset allocation model. Here's the key that most advisors won't mention: your advisor's goal should be to get better returns with less risk than the benchmarks identified in your asset allocation model. Matching it or getting "close enough" is not acceptable. You could do that on your own with index funds at a dramatically lower cost.

Your Asset Allocation Model

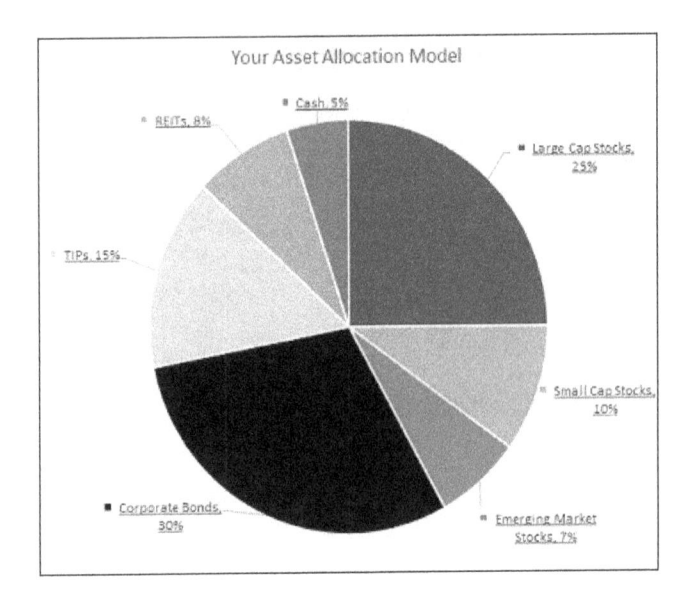

- Cash, 5%
- REITs, 8%
- Large Cap Stocks, 25%
- TIPs, 15%
- Small Cap Stocks, 10%
- Corporate Bonds, 30%
- Emerging Market Stocks, 7%

Portfolio Growth Chart

This next chart is also usually standard in performance reviews. It is a chart that shows the growth of the portfolio along with the growth of popular stock or bond indexes. While informative about general market conditions and their effect on your portfolio's returns, the chart actually tells you nothing about the skill with which your money was invested. Unfortunately, it is standard procedure in the vast majority of performance reviews produced by retail financial advisors.

The problem this represents is called *improper benchmarking*. Your portfolio does not share the risk/return characteristics of the indexes shown on the

A DEEPER DIVE INTO INVESTMENT REPORTING

chart. Therefore, it's not a relevant comparison and is misleading..

It's kind of like being in college and your report card shows your grade from an algebra class, and next to it you see the average grades of the French literature class taught next door. While it might look interesting at first glance, it really gives you no useful feedback on your performance at all.

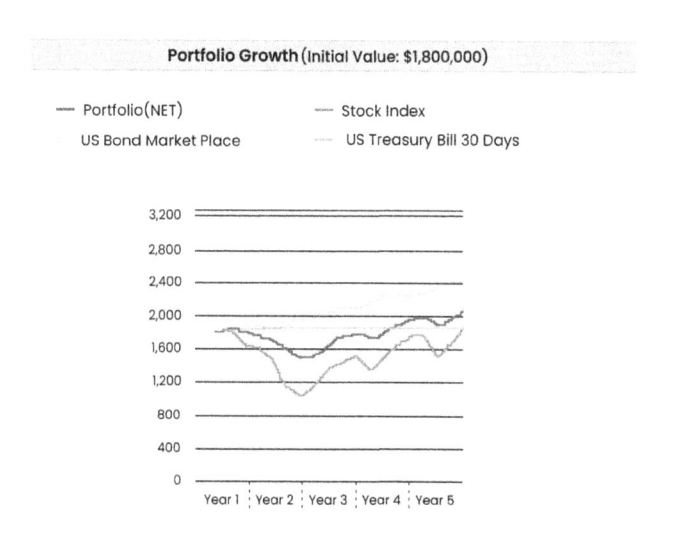

Portfolio Growth (Initial Value: $1,800,000)

- Portfolio(NET)
- US Bond Market Place
- Stock Index
- US Treasury Bill 30 Days

Cumulative Performance Chart

Next up, you'll often find a cumulative performance chart. As you might expect, this graph shows the growth of your portfolio compared to a benchmark index. In this case, the benchmark is the correct one for this specific portfolio because both have the same risk and return goals. However, what we don't know is if the investments in the actual portfolio were exposed to more or less risk to generate the returns shown here. (That requires a separate risk study, which we will get to later.)

Historical Performance

— Your Portfolio
— Portfolio Benchmark

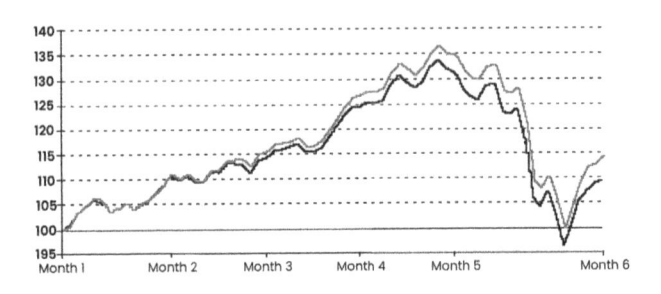

Annual Performance

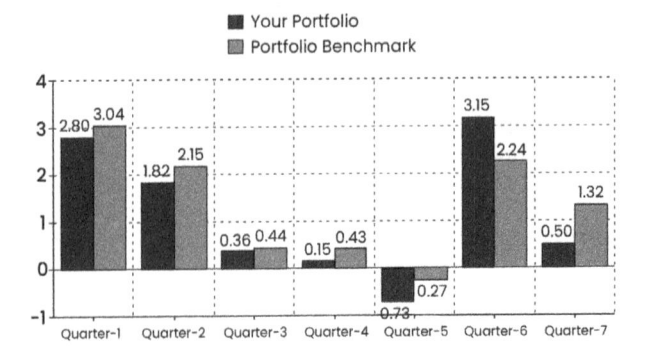

■ Your Portfolio
■ Portfolio Benchmark

Quarter	Your Portfolio	Portfolio Benchmark
Quarter-1	2.80	3.04
Quarter-2	1.82	2.15
Quarter-3	0.36	0.44
Quarter-4	0.15	0.43
Quarter-5	-0.73	0.27
Quarter-6	3.15	2.24
Quarter-7	0.50	1.32

Charts Common in Institutional Reporting

So far, you're getting some information, but much of it is limited in actual usefulness. Let's move on to what you really *should* see. The studies and charts from this point forward usually are only available to institutional investors.

If your financial advisor provides this level of analysis for your annual performance review, they are on the right track. But don't forget, always have an independent third party produce your yearly performance review (or make sure the report is certified to be GIPS® compliant). It is the only way to guarantee the report uses accurate data and gives you a clear picture of what actually happened with your money.

Annual Performance (Time-Based Bar) Chart

This next chart shows return performance but displayed in time periods rather than as a continual line.

Everybody wants great returns. But if you take extra risk to generate those returns, your portfolio could be exposed to more significant downside moves when markets pull back. And nobody wants to take losses that are larger than necessary. One method to visualize the risk/return of your portfolio versus the risk/return of specific markets is a time analysis such as this.

Risk vs. Return Analysis

Ⓐ Your Portfolio net of fees
◆ Your Benchmark with fees

Risk vs. Return Analysis

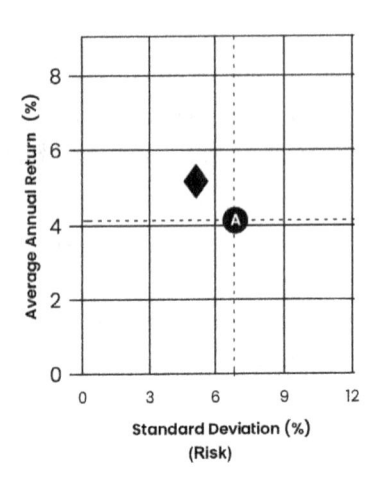

[Scatter plot: Average Annual Return (%) vs. Standard Deviation (%) (Risk). Benchmark ◆ at approximately (5, 5); Portfolio Ⓐ at approximately (7, 4).]

Risk Analysis Charts

So how do you know conclusively if your portfolio is taking on more or less risk than you agreed to when you accepted the asset allocation model as your benchmark? This is critical since taking too much risk to generate benchmark returns is a sign of a poorly managed portfolio. On the flip side, taking too little risk could mean not achieving your goals. This risk can be significant in times of increasing inflation, so this is important.

Annual Rolling Risk

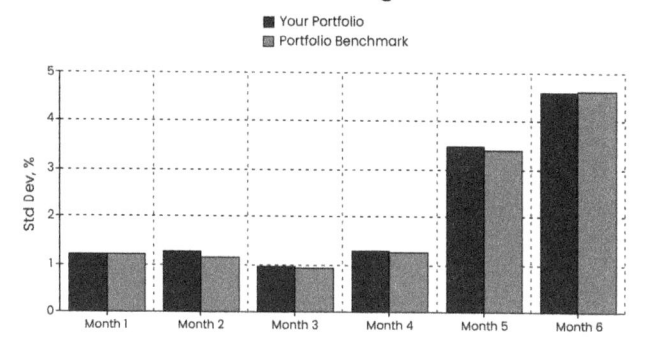

■ Your Portfolio
▫ Portfolio Benchmark

Up Capture / Down Capture Chart

One of the most insightful studies concerning the quality of your portfolio management is the up capture / down capture chart. The "up capture" number represents how much of the benchmark returns your portfolio captures when the portfolio benchmark increases. The "down capture" number represents how much of the benchmark returns your portfolio captures when the benchmark declines in value. What should you look for? You want to see an up-capture figure larger than the downside capture. Be aware that either figure can exceed 100 percent.

Up/Down Capture Ratio

▲ Your Portfolio

[Chart: Up Market Capture Ratio, % (y-axis, 0–100) vs Down Market Capture Ratio, % (x-axis, 0–120). A triangle marker is plotted near (105, 98).]

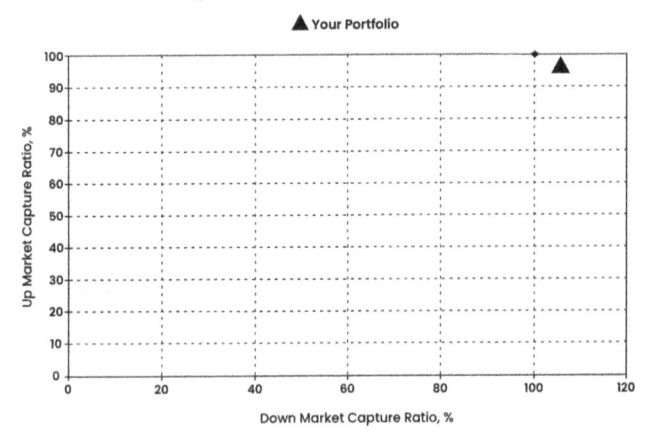

Information Ratio Chart

Next, the Information Ratio chart measures how much value has been added by the investment manager per the corresponding unit of risk. It's a bit technical, but here's a shortcut: bars above the zero line are desirable.

As a useful exercise, count the number of times the bar appears above the zero line. Then, divide that number by the number of times the bar appears below the zero line. You are looking for the result to be greater than one.

Information Ratio

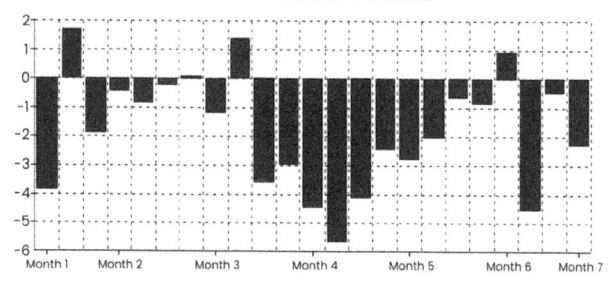

Sharpe Ratio Chart

Next, we have the Sharpe ratio, developed by William Sharpe in 1966.[43] You might have seen this term if you were reading up on mutual fund performance. In general terms, the Sharpe ratio tells you if your portfolio returns are due to skilled investment management or simply taking excess risk. A good Sharpe ratio is greater than one. Sharpe ratios over two and approaching three are considered excellent.

The batting average is a measurement of how often your portfolio's returns beat the returns of the assigned benchmark. It's a consistency metric. It will tell you if excess returns resulted from just a few lucky months or were achieved consistently. Institutional investors like to see a batting average above 0.5.

---

[43] Nick Lioudis, "Understanding the Sharpe Ratio," Investopedia, April 30, 2021, https://www.investopedia.com/articles/07/sharpe_ratio.asp.

- Sharpe Ratio
- Batting Average

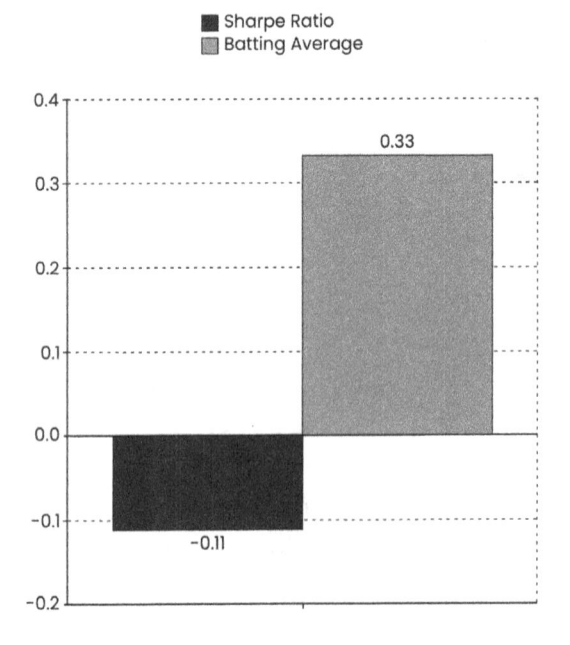

Bar chart values: Sharpe Ratio = -0.11; Batting Average = 0.33

That's our deeper dive into reporting. There's just one last concept to discuss.

Understanding Alpha and Beta

These previous examples of institutional analysis involve the concepts of alpha and beta. Alpha is defined as a measure of performance on a risk-adjusted basis. You want to see your advisor generating an alpha above zero. That means they are adding value on a risk-adjusted basis. In other words, they are not just swinging for the fences with your money.

Beta is the tendency of a portfolio's returns to respond

A DEEPER DIVE INTO INVESTMENT REPORTING

to the benchmarks. It is a measure of volatility. If your portfolio has a beta of less than one, that usually means your portfolio returns will be less volatile than that of the benchmarks. The reverse is true if the beta is greater than one. High beta portfolios (or investments) often have exaggerated swings since they tend to move more than the market does. Typically, a skilled portfolio manager will strive for a beta of less than one as long as return performance is unaffected.

Yes, these are technical terms, but it can be helpful to at least be aware of them. The saying in the institutional office is that "negative alpha gets you fired." And high beta? That often is the stuff that keeps investors awake at night, when your portfolio swings far more than the rest of the market.

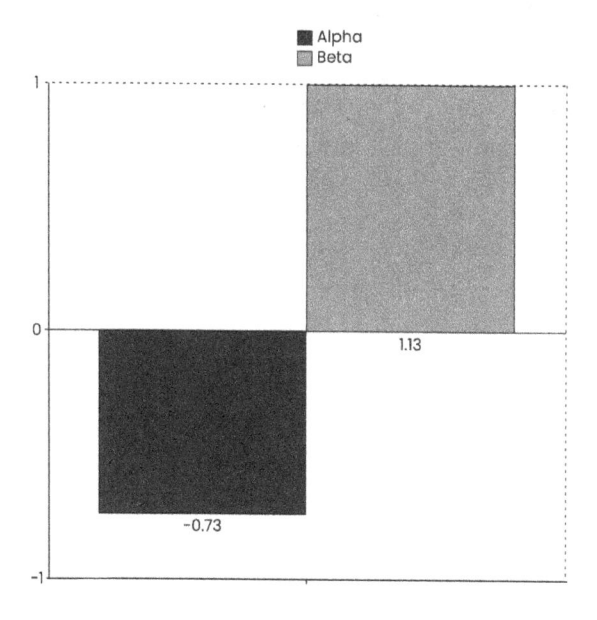

You are now better equipped

It is likely you now are far better equipped to understand the nature of your relationship with your financial advisor. Make no mistake - a skilled financial advisor is worth every penny they earn. But how can you tell if your account is benefitting from your advisor's investing advice? Is it possible their fees are simply acting as a performance drag? We know from a bellwether industry study that 75 percent of investors would be interested in using a third-party performance verification service if available.

This is exactly why we are starting FinancialAdvisorCheck.com.

We want to provide investors with a third-party option they can trust, so they can feel confident that their money is in good hands.

Your results are never shared. It's just between us - your advisor, and their firm, will never know.

ACKNOWLEDGMENTS

As you've read in the preceding chapters, the genesis for this book is a tragedy that no one should go through. Unless you have had it happen to you, you cannot fathom the pain.

That event motivated me to enter the investment industry and fueled my efforts to bring accountability to the people on its front lines – retail financial advisors and their firms' marketing departments.

It would be a serious mistake to think that this book condemns retail financial advisors. On the contrary. I believe that an investor's greatest asset is a skilled financial advisor. Any suggestion to the contrary is in error.

As the Covid19 lockdown progressed, and my honey-do list disappeared, I set out to write this book based on my experiences in the industry. In the beginning my muse(s) were my cousins - Perry and Nick. When this book hits the shelves, I doubt any two people will be more surprised, but it is due to them that I gained the confidence to write it.

At about the halfway point, it was clear that I'd need some help. My first stroke of good (great) luck came in finding Jeanne Klimowski. Not only is she a talented writer, but her knowledge of investment industry practices exceeded all my expectations. She is a true professional, and a real team player without whom this effort could have not come to fruition.

After the content was locked, I set out to publish. The ladies at Book Launchers have my gratitude. They were like professional guides in the African wild. In a word - comforting. Where I had questions, they had answers. Where I had hesitation, they had reason and motivation. Elissa and Nicole – thanks for everything. You are marvelous.

But none of this would have been possible without my wife Addie. On top of a demanding job, she puts up with my eccentricities and the self-imposed isolation a writer often unwittingly imposes upon themself. She is our family's rock of Gibraltar and the love of my life.

This book does have a purpose and I hope it is one that you will become a part of. My company has developed a mobile app (Financial Advisor Check) to bring retail investors, for free, a level of accountability and transparency that should be the norm, but unfortunately is restricted to the very wealthy.

ACKNOWLEDGMENTS

The Wall Street firms that advise you and that make up this industry are powerful and chock full of conflicts of interest. Fortunately, they are powerless to stop you from demanding accountability and utilizing the tools needed to achieve that goal. The only resistance to forcing transparency on Wall Street is your hesitancy.

We made the app to function without alerting your brokerage. The results are just between us.

I look forward to helping you change the industry and watching you retire sooner and richer.

Norman D. Pappous

CPSIA information can be obtained
at www.ICGtesting.com
Printed in the USA
LVHW020839221022
731316LV00007B/580